Introduction to the Mac
Backups, Apps & Settings

MacOS 13 Ventura Edition

© 2023 iTandCoffee

Special Sales and Supply Queries

For any information about buying this title in bulk quantities, or for supply of this title for educational or fund-raising purposes, contact iTandCoffee on **1300 885 420** or email **enquiry@itandcoffee.com.au**.

iTandCoffee classes and private appointments

For queries about classes and private appointments with iTandCoffee, call **1300 885 420** or email **enquiry@itandcoffee.com.au**.

iTandCoffee operates in and around Camberwell, Victoria in Australia.

Introducing iTandCoffee ...

iTandCoffee is a Melbourne-based business that was founded in 2012, by IT professional Lynette Coulston.

Lynette and the staff at iTandCoffee have a passion for helping others - especially women of all ages - to enter and navigate the new, and often daunting, world of technology and to utilise technology to make life easier, not harder!

At iTandCoffee, **patience is our virtue.**

You'll find a welcoming smile, a relaxed cup of tea or coffee, and a genuine enthusiasm for helping you to gain the confidence to use and enjoy your technology.

With personalised appointments and small, friendly classes – either remotely, in our bright, comfortable, cafe-style space or at your own place - we offer a brand of technology support and education that is so hard to find.

At iTandCoffee, you won't find young 'techies' who speak in a foreign language and move at a pace that leaves you floundering and 'bamboozled'!

Our focus is on helping you to use your technology in a way that enhances your personal and/or professional life – to feel more informed, organised, connected and entertained!

Call on iTandCoffee for help with all sorts of technology – Apple, Windows, Android, iCloud, Evernote, OneDrive, Office 365, Dropbox, all sorts of other Apps, getting you set up on the internet, setting up a printer, and so much more.

Introducing iTandCoffee …

If you are in small business, iTandCoffee has can help in so many ways – with amazing affordable solutions for your business information needs and marketing.

Here are just some of the topics covered in our regular classes:

- Microsoft Office Products and Microsoft 365 – OneDrive, Word, Excel, PowerPoint
- Introduction to the iPad and iPhone
- A Guided Tour of the Apple Watch
- Bring your Busy Life under Control using your technology.
- Getting to know your Mac and The Photos app on the Mac
- Understanding and using iCloud
- An Organised Life with Evernote
- Taking and Managing photos on the iPhone and iPad
- Managing Photos on a Windows computer
- Windows basics
- Travel with your iPad, iPhone and other technology.
- Keeping kids safe on the iPad, iPhone and iPod Touch.
- Staying Safe Online
- Making the most of your personal technology in your business

The iTandCoffee website (itandcoffee.com.au) offers a wide variety of resources for those brave enough to venture online to learn more: handy hints for iPad, iPhone and Mac; videos and slideshows of iTandCoffee classes; guides on a range of topics; a blog covering all sorts of topical events.

We also produce a regular Handy Hint newsletter full of information that is of interest to our clients and subscribers.

Hopefully, that gives you a bit of a picture of iTandCoffee and what we are about. Please don't hesitate to contact iTandCoffee to discuss our services or to make a booking.

We hope you enjoy this guide and find its contents informative and useful. Please feel free to offer feedback at feedback@itandcoffee.com.au.

Regards,

Lynette Coulston (iTandCoffee Founder)

Introduction to the Mac

Backups, Apps & Settings

TABLE OF CONTENTS

Introduction to the Mac

Backups, Apps & Settings

TABLE OF CONTENTS (cont.)

Introduction to the Mac

Backups, Apps & Settings

TABLE OF CONTENTS (cont.)

Introduction to the Mac
Backups, Apps & Settings
TABLE OF CONTENTS (cont.)

Before we start

About this guide

In this third guide of the **Introduction to the Mac** series, we focus on three key areas – Backups, Apps and Settings.

We look at how to protect yourself from the loss of your valuable data and photos, how to 'fine-tune', manage and monitor your Mac's apps, and we take a look at some of the key apps – with some great tips for getting more from these great built-in apps.

In looking at these apps, we do not seek to provide a comprehensive training guide on how to use the apps, but rather to help you find the features that you may not otherwise realise are available – features that can really enhance your use of the App.

A great companion to this guide – providing more detailed instruction on these apps – is our online **Mastering the Mac** set of tutorials, available on the iTandCoffee Website.

Visit www.itandcoffee.com.au/apple-mac-videos for more information.

Click, Double-click and Right-Click

Throughout this guide, we will often refer to the 'Click' and 'Right-click' gestures.

Refer to Part 1 of this series of **Introduction to the Mac** guides, called **A Guided Tour**, for more details of how to set up your **Mouse and Trackpad** in **System Settings** to support your preferences for these gestures.

When we refer to 'Click', we are talking about the standard single left-click on the Mouse or a single-finger click on the main area of the Trackpad. 'Double-click' means two 'clicks' in quick succession.

(Note. This assumes a 'right-handed' setup for your Mouse! You can set up your Mouse to switch sides for the 'click' and 'right-click' gestures if you are left-handed. See **A Guided Tour** for more on this.)

This 'click' and 'double-click' could instead be a 'tap' or 'double-tap' if you have enabled this feature in the **System Settings** for your **Mouse** or **Trackpad**.

Where there are references to the **'right-click'** gesture, this is referring the 'right-click on the Mouse' gesture – called the **secondary click** in **System Settings -> Mouse,** or **Trackpad**.

This the same gesture as the **Control-click** keyboard shortcut, the **two-finger click** gesture on the trackpad, and the **bottom right corner click** gesture on the trackpad (if you have chosen this instead of the 'two-finger click').

Before we start

In some places in the document, we mention all of the 'secondary click' gestures when we refer to 'right-click'. But in cases were where we only mention the 'right-click', please substitute the gesture that applies on your own Mac.

Scrolling

For those of you who are using a MacBook and its Trackpad, don't forget that scrolling up and down is achieved by dragging two fingers up and down on your trackpad, and one finger up and down on your Magic Mouse.

Refer to the guide **A Guided Tour** for more details about setting up your Mac's Trackpad gestures.

New in macOS Ventura

Throughout this document, we refer to various changes that have arrived with macOS Ventura. Below are specific sections that discuss some of the more significant changes (as well as the corresponding page number).

Let's talk Backups -
Time Machine

Our Mac computers, like any other computer, usually end up holding a huge amount of information and files that are important to us – photos, work documents, assignments, and other valuable content.

It is therefore very important to ensure that the content stored on the Mac is also saved somewhere else as a '*backup*'.

A **backup** is the process of copying the contents of your computer to a separate device or storage area so that, should something happen to your computer, you can 'restore' this backup and continue where you left off – without the loss of any data or apps.

"Doesn't iCloud back up my Mac?"

Many people have the misconception that iCloud will look after backing up of their Mac, just as it can do for their iPad and iPhone.

This is not the case - **iCloud does not back up your Mac**.

While it may 'synchronise' at least some of your data, it is not looking after the backup of <u>all</u> files that are stored in <u>all</u> areas of your Mac. (Note. In saying this, you may be using iCloud to 'sync' your Documents and Desktop folders.)

If your Mac suffers a crash, is broken, or is stolen, you may lose precious information if you have failed to perform a regular backup.

A backup can also allow you to retrieve an individual file that has been mistakenly deleted or modified. An entire folder can be retrieved from a backup, should this ever be necessary.

So, how do I back up my Mac?

Fortunately, Apple makes it extremely easy for you to back up your Mac.

Your Mac includes a built-in feature called '**Time Machine**' that is very easy to set up.

Let's Talk Backups - Time Machine

Time Machine Settings have moved in macOS Ventura

To see the options associated with **Time Machine** and set it up, visit **System Settings -> General -> Time Machine**.

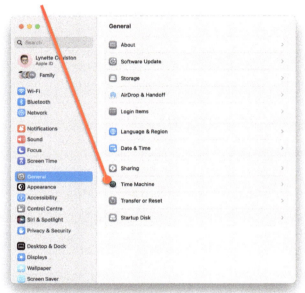

What do I backup to?

Backups can be to an 'External Hard Drive' like that shown below left, which plugs in to a USB port on your Mac.

They can also be to a Wi-Fi enabled external drive, such as Apple's **Time Capsule**, although this device is no longer produced by Apple. (We won't cover Time Capsule or wireless backups in this guide. Ask **iTandCoffee** if you need help with this.)

Let's Talk Backups - Time Machine

Connecting a new backup device (changed in macOS Ventura)

The first time that you plug in such a portable external hard drive, you will be asked to **Allow** that device to connect to your Mac.

You may see the below message.

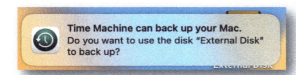

Hover the pointer over this message, and choose **Options** when it appears, then **Set Up Disk** (if you do want to use the external drive for this purpose).

If no such message appears after you plug in the device, go to **System Settings -> General -> Time Machine** and choose **Add Backup Disk.**

Let's Talk Backups - Time Machine

If you already have another device set up for backups (as showing in the image below), click the + to add another device.

You will then be presented with another screen for setting up the backup – one that provides the option to **Encrypt Backup**.

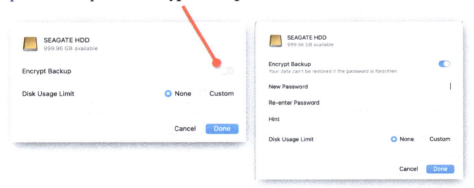

It is a good idea to turn this feature on, so that the content of your backup will be protected from unauthorised access.

If you turn on **Encrypt Backup**, you will be required to also provide a password (and re-enter to confirm it).

This password will be used to scramble (encrypt) the backup data so that it can only be read by someone who provides the correct password. Of course, it is essential that you don't forget this password.

Make sure you include a Hint in the field provided – which should, of course, be something that is obscure enough that an unauthorised person cannot guess the password from it.

Let's Talk Backups - Time Machine

When you choose **Done,** the external device will be prepared and, when done, the external device will appear in the list of Time Machine devices (as shown in the below example. The first backup will start automatically after about a minute.

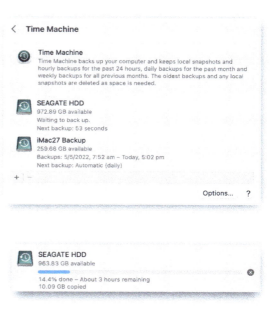

This first backup will usually take quite a bit of time, as it usually needs to perform a backup of a large amount of data. For example, a backup I ran recently ran for 12 hours.

Subsequent backups will not take nearly as long, as they will only backup any files that are new or changed since the last backup.

An important warning when setting up a backup

<u>If you use an external hard drive with data already on it</u>, you may lose all this data if you decide to use this drive as your Time Machine backup.

If the drive needs to be reformatted by Time Machine, this will completely wipe all data from that hard drive first.

So, it is recommended to only use an already-used hard drive if you are not concerned about losing the data that it contains (or if you know the drive is already formatted for Mac backups).

How often does Time Machine back up?

Once **Time Machine** is turned on and set up, your Mac will, by default, be backed up every hour whenever the external hard drive is connected.

It is not necessary to tell your Mac when to do the backup – it will happen automatically.

As discussed on the next page, the frequency can now be customised in macOS Ventura

Let's Talk Backups - Time Machine

Choose an alternative backup frequency (macOS Ventura)

If you want to choose an alternative frequency for your backups, click the **Options** button in the **Time Machine** option of **System Settings**

A new option is available in Ventura – **Back up frequency**. Click this field to see the options available and click to choose an alternative.

The options available are now Manually, Every Hour, Every Day and Every Week.

This is especially handy if, like me, you use Cloud storage for most of your important files, and perhaps don't need hourly backups.

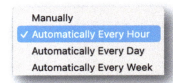

Are all backups kept forever?

Backups are not kept forever – there would not be enough room on any hard drive for this to be possible.

Your Time Machine will keep hourly backups for the last 24 hours (assuming you are doing hourly backups), then daily backups for the last 30 days (if you are doing at least daily backups), then weekly backups after that.

When the backup hard drive fills, some intermediate backups will be automatically removed to make way for a new backup.

Viewing backup progress (change in macOS Ventura)

The easiest way to keep track of the progress of your backup/s is to include the **Time Machine** icon in the top Menu Bar on your Mac. The way in which you enable the icon in the Menu bar has changed in macOS Ventura

Let's Talk Backups - Time Machine

This is achieved by visiting the **Control Centre** option of **System Settings**.

The very last option in Control Centre is **Time Machine**. Click the value that is showing there and change it to **Show in Menu Bar**.

The symbol  will be then visible in the status bar. Click it to see the backup progress, or, if no backup is in progress, when the last backup was completed.

You will also see you have to option to **Back Up Now**, to force a backup at any time (assuming the backup hard drive is plugged in).

Let's Talk Backups - Time Machine

Viewing your backups

To view your backups – and perhaps retrieve a file or folder that was backed up on a past date, click on the Time Machine symbol in the status bar at top right, then click **Browse Time Machine Backups**.

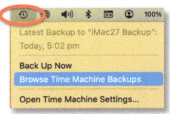

A 3-D looking screen will appear, showing a stack of Finder windows, and some 'dates' over on the right-hand side.

Click on any of the dates on the right to go back to that date and view the files in Finder, as they were at that date.

Or use the arrows on the right-hand side of the 'stack' of windows to move back and forward through the backups – or click on a date in the timeline that shows on the right side.

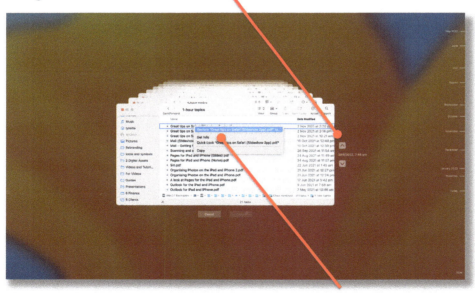

If you find the file or folder that needs to be 'restored', right-click on it (or two-finger click, if this is your 'secondary click' gesture), choose the **Restore** option and choose where to restore that file (or folder). Or click to select it, then choose the **Restore** button beneath the windows.

Choose **Cancel** to exit your Time Machine and return to your normal screen.

Another look at System Settings

As we already touched on in Part 1 of this series of guides, **System Settings** on your Mac is the equivalent of the **Control Panel** on a Windows computer (for those of you who come from a Windows background) or the **Settings** app on an iPhone and iPad. As already mentioned, System Settings was called System Preferences prior to macOS Ventura.

System Settings allows for the management of system wide settings and preferences on the Mac. It is accessed from the Apple menu at top left:

 -> **System Settings**

or from the **System Settings** app in the Dock.

Let's take a quick look at a few key areas of System Settings, areas that we didn't look at in Part 1 of this series of guides, called **A Guided Tour.**

Don't be afraid to explore your System Settings, as you will find a huge array of settings that can make your Mac work even better for you.

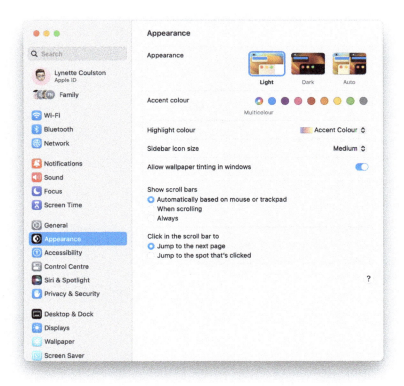

Another look at System Settings

Set up Users & List and Parental Controls

The **Users & Groups** option in System Settings is the area that allows for the set-up of separate User accounts for your children and other users of the Mac, so that you can 'rope off' your own account, and (if required), set limitations on what other users can do and access on the Mac (called Parental Controls).

To add a new user, choose the **Add Account ...** option.

You will be asked to provide your administrator account credentials to continue.

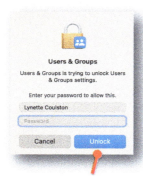

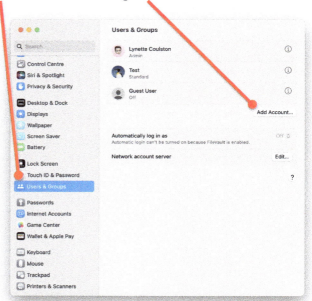

Enter your account's password, then **Unlock**.

Fill in the new user's details and assign a password (or choose to use the new user's iCloud password to unlock that user account).

The **New Account** option at the top of the 'new user' screen allows for the selection of the account's 'type'. This will determine what the user is able to do, use and see.

16

Another look at System Settings

Only choose **Administrator** for a user that you wish to give them full control of the computer.

Otherwise, choose **Standard**.

The **Sharing Only** option allows for the creation of an account that simply shares certain files and folders from another account, and the List option allows controlling of sharing for a set of accounts. We won't go into these areas as part of this guide.

Setting up an account with Parental Controls

With the arrival of macOS Catalina in 2019, the way that you set up an account for a child – one that has age-appropriate Parental Controls – changed.

The new **Screen Time** option has extended the range of options that are available for parents who want to manage their child's usage of the Mac.

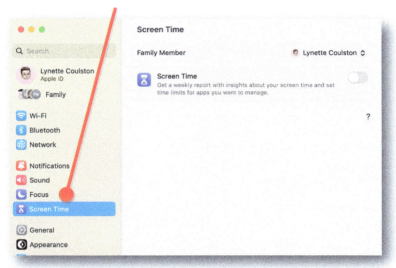

We won't cover this topic in detail as part of this guide, as it is the subject of a separate iTandCoffee guide – except to say that, if you want to be able to parentally control your child's use of the Mac, you must set up an 'Administrator' account for yourself, then a 'Standard' account for the child.

This will then allow you to set up the Screen Time controls for the child's user account and set a Screen Time password that only YOU know, to protect your child.

Another look at System Settings

Manage Printers & Scanners

The **Printers & Scanners** option is the at the very end of the list of main **System Settings** options. It allows for the addition of a new printer (or scanner).

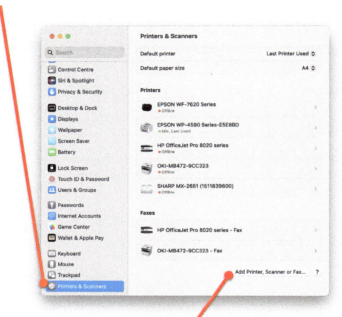

To set up a new printer, chose the **Add Printer, Scanner or Fax ...** button at the bottom.

The **Add** window will appear, showing a list of any printers that your Mac can 'see' – either because they are attached to the Mac via a USB cable, or because they are Wi-Fi printers attached to the same Wi-Fi network as the Mac.

Click on the applicable printer and choose **Add**. Usually, it's that simple!

Another look at System Settings

To remove a printer that you no longer need, click on it in the list of available printers to see the below screen. Choose **Remove Printer**.

This screen also provides the option to **Set Default Printer** – to choose this printer as the default to use whenever Print is chosen. This can then be changed on a case-by-case basis.

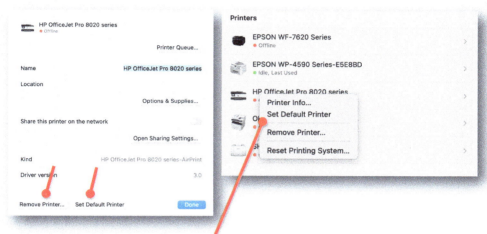

Another way of managing the printers in the list is to right-click on any entry to see several options, including **Remove Printer** and **Set Default Printer**.

Set up Internet Accounts

Your email accounts like Gmail, Outlook, Yahoo, Exchange, etc. are set up in the option **Internet Accounts**.

For IMAP and Exchange email addresses hosted by Microsoft, Google, Yahoo, Apple, etc – i.e. email addresses that are 'cloud based' and able to be synchronised between all your devices – this is where you can choose what features of your account you want to use: Calendar, Contacts, Reminders, Notes and more (depending on what the account offers).

Click on any existing account in the list to view these options.

Another look at System Settings

Just 'tick' those features that you wish to turn on.

To add a new email account, choose the **Add Account ...** option (see image at bottom of previous page).

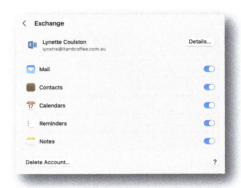

Select the type of account you wish to add, the follow the instructions to sign in to the account and add it. (We won't go into this further here.)

Set up iCloud on your Mac

iCloud is normally set up as part of the process of setting up your Mac, either initially or when you perform an upgrade.

If you would like your key information on your Mac to synchronise with that same information on your iPad and iPhone – for example, your Contacts, Calendars, Reminders, Notes and more – you must sign in to your iCloud account on both your mobile devices AND on your Mac.

The first option (Apple ID) in **System Settings** is where your iCloud setup for Mac is managed. If you are already signed in to iCloud, this item in the sidebar will reflect your name.

If you are not signed in, select this option and sign in to your Apple account.

The iCloud option is where you choose what data in your iCloud should sync to and from this Mac.

Another look at System Settings

Ensure that each type of data that you wish to synchronise using iCloud is turn 'On' (circle is on the right side, and left is blue). Click on right side to move the circle if any option you require is turned off.

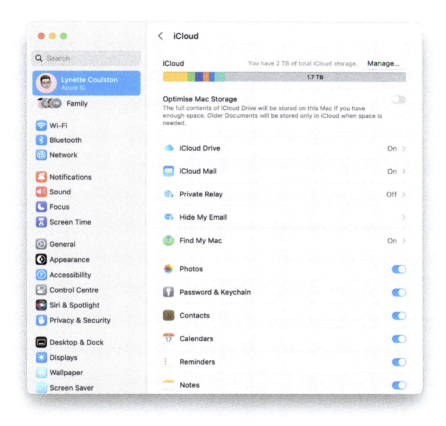

Other options – such as iCloud Drive, your iCloud Mail, privacy features relating to Mail, and Find My Mac can also be managed from here. And you can see and manage your iCloud storage usage.

For a full description of iCloud and the options shown in this area of System Settings, see the separate guide by iTandCoffee, called **The Comprehensive Guide to iCloud**.

Application Settings

New name for App Preferences in macOS Ventura

While the **System Settings** area allows for the setting of your system-wide preferences on the Mac, as we have already mentioned in parts 1 and 2 of this series that there are also **Settings** associated with each individual App on your Mac. (Note. There are a few exceptions to this rule.)

For Windows users, these Settings are the equivalent of 'Properties' or 'Options' for the App.)

Before macOS Ventura, these Settings were referred to as Preferences.

Viewing an Apps Settings

Whenever an app is the 'currently active' app, its name and menu will always appear alongside the at the top left – perhaps even if there are not currently any windows showing for that app.

To view and set up the settings/preferences for a particular App, click on the <u>name of the App</u> (on the right of the), then choose **Settings** from drop-down list.

Alternatively, choose ⌘, (Command-comma) which will also bring up the Settings for the app.

As an example, the **Settings** for the **Music** app (shown on right) provide a range of options along the top, which then include lots of sub-options to choose from.

Don't be afraid to explore the Settings associated with each of the Apps that you use.

Managing Apps and Windows

The importance of the Black Dots

Quite often, you will find that you have several Apps running at the same time on your Mac. The apps that are currently running are indicated in the **Dock** with a **black dot** underneath them.

As already discussed in part 1 of this series of guides, it is essential to keep the number of apps that are currently running under control, ensuring that those that are not being used are not left open and consuming unnecessary resources of the Mac. Right click on any app in the dock that shows a black dot and choose Quit to fully close it.

Multi-window Apps

It is essential to understand the concept of App Windows and how to manage them on your Mac. Otherwise, they can tend to 'breed'!

Most apps can have multiple active windows. As an example, there could be multiple Finder windows open at the same time and multiple Pages documents open as separate windows at the same time. These Windows can be viewed in different ways - re-sized, minimised and individually closed.

The Traffic lights

When an App is the currently active app, a set of what I call 'Traffic Lights' appear at the top left of the app window.

When the window is not active, these Traffic Lights will be grey.

In summary, these Traffic Lights have the following meaning

- **Red = Close** the active Window
- **Yellow = Minimise** the Window
- **Green = Expand/Contract** the size of the window to/from full screen (or split screen mode)

Red Light

As mentioned earlier, it is important to realize that many apps allow you to open multiple windows for the App. If an app is a 'multi-window' app, then clicking the Red Light will only close the Window, and not necessarily close the App.

Managing Apps and Windows

Some Apps are single-window apps – for example, the App Store and Notes. In such cases, clicking the Red Light on a 'single-window' app will close the Window AND the App.

Yellow Light

Clicking the Yellow light will minimize the Window into the Dock (or, depending on System Settings, into the 'Stacks' area to the left of the trash can).

Go to **System Settings -> Desktop & Dock** to choose where 'minimised' Windows go – ie. whether they appear individually in the 'Stacks area' on the right side of the Dock, near the Trash; or whether they are **Minimised into the application icon**.

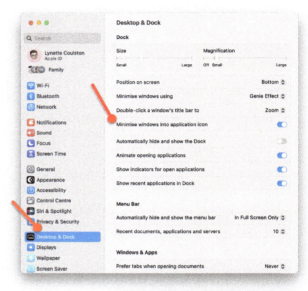

To open the minimised window again, just click on the App in the Dock or, if it is minimized to the 'Stacks area', click on the 'thumbnail' (small image) for the window.

If you have minimised multiple windows for the same App, you can also right-click on the app in the Dock and see the list of open windows at the top. For example, I currently have three Word documents open. Simply click to window you wish to to make that window the active window.

A word of caution about turning off the **Minimise windows into application icon** option: you can end up with a lot of minimised app windows in the Dock, which can make your other app icons very small. A client of iTandCoffee recently had this issue and could no longer make out the tiny app icons in the Dock. By closing the app and changing the 'Minimise' setting we resolved this (at first) puzzling issue.

Managing Apps and Windows

Green light

The Green light can do multiple things.

Full screen vs Partial screen modes

When a Window is showing in a 'partial screen' mode (i.e. it is not taking up the entire screen), a quick click on the green dot will put the window into Full Screen mode.

In **Full Screen mode**, the Dock disappears, as does the menu and status bar at the top (unless a System Setting specifies otherwise).

To make the Dock appear while in this full screen mode, hover the 'cursor' at the very bottom of the screen.

To make the menu/status bar appear, hover the cursor at the very top of the screen.

If you want the menu bar to always be visible in full screen mode, choose **Never** for **System Settings -> Desktop & Dock -> Automatically hide and show the menu bar**.

The way in which you exit **'full screen'** depends on the App you are running in this mode.

For Apple and many third-party apps, simply **press the Esc key** (top left key) to exit full screen mode.

Alternatively, hover the cursor near the top left to see  and **click the Green dot**.

For some older 'non-Apple' apps, it may be necessary to hover the cursor near top right and click   when it appears.

Managing Apps and Windows

Split Screen Mode

Another function of the Green Light is to put your screen into 'split screen' mode.

This only applies to Apple Apps, and newer versions of third-party apps that have been built to enable this feature.

To activate 'Split Screen Mode', just **hover over the green dot** to see a set of options appear – to choose between full screen mode, or to enter 'split screen mode', with the app window taking over the left or right side of the screen.

You can then choose which other currently running app you wish to see on the alternative side of the screen.

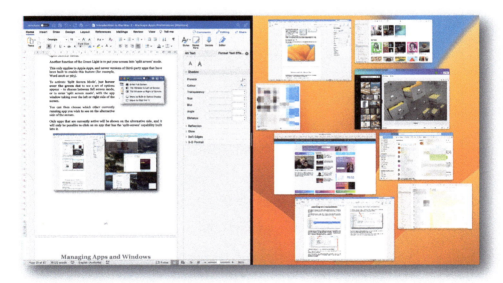

Managing Apps and Windows

Only apps that are currently active will be shown on the alternative side, and it will only be possible to click on an app that has the 'split-screen' capability built into it.

Simply click on the applicable App that you wish to fill that other part of screen.

To exit this Split Screen mode, hover the cursor up at the very top and click for the Window that you wish to take out of this mode (or press Esc).

The app on which the cursor was positioned when you exit Split Screen mode will be the active app (now in part-screen mode) and the other app will remain in 'full screen mode' – but on another 'virtual desktop'. (We will briefly cover the concept

Managing Apps and Windows

of multiple Desktops shortly, including how to move between them and how to choose what apps appear on what desktop using Mission Control 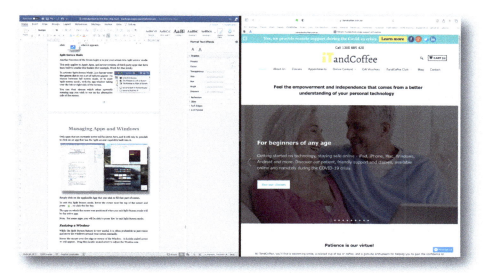 .)

Resizing a Window

While the Split Screen feature is very useful, it is often preferable to just resize and move the windows around your screen manually.

As already covered in Part 2 – in relation to Finder - hover the mouse over the edge or corner of the Window. A double-ended arrow ↔ will appear. Drag this double-ended arrow to adjust the Window size.

Moving a Window

As also covered in Part 2, moving a Window around the screen involves clicking in the vicinity of the 'traffic lights' – I recommend just to the right of these icons - and dragging the window to its new position.

In fact, clicking anywhere that is in line horizontally with those traffic lights (and dragging) will allow you to move the window.

Managing Apps and Windows

Multiple Desktops for your Windows

Your Mac includes a capability to organise your app windows onto different virtual Desktops. This is like having multiple displays for your Mac, each showing different apps/windows.

It is your Mission Control (described in Part 1 of this series – called A Guided Tour) that allows you to see and manage these Desktops.

If you are currently viewing one of the desktops and wish to view another 'desktop, use the keyboard shortcut Control-▶ to move one desktop to the right, and Control-◀ to move to the left. Depending on your Mouse and/or Trackpad settings, you can also use gestures to move between desktops (two finger swipe left or right on Mouse, three finger swipe left or right on Trackpad).

Or to view and manage your desktops using Mission Control

- click the Mission Control app in the Dock,

- press the F3 key

- use the keyboard shortcut Control-◻.

The The desktops show as icons along the top bar. While in this view,

- Drag apps from the currently visible desktop onto a different desktop if required.

Managing Apps and Windows

- Use the same gestures as described earlier for switching between desktops while in Mission Control – i.e. Control- to move one desktop to the right, and Control- to move to the left; or depending on your Mouse and/or Trackpad settings, you can also use gestures to move between desktops (two finger swipe left or right on Mouse, three finger swipe left or right on Trackpad.)

- Click on any desktop to switch to it.

- Drag the desktop images (as they appear along the top) to re-order.

- Hover over any desktop to see an ⊗ at top left and to remove it (and merge its app windows into the first previous desktop).

- Create a new desktop by hovering over the bar at top and choosing the + that appears at right end.

If you have more than one monitor attached to your Mac, each monitor will have its own set of desktops (unless you have chosen to 'mirror' your displays).

For settings relating to other monitors/displays, visit **System Settings -> Displays**.

Handy Shortcuts for managing apps

Here are some handy ways of switching between and managing the apps that are running and appearing in the Dock.

Command-Tab

Switch between your currently running apps by holding down the Command key and pressing Tab key at the same time – multiple times, if necessary, to switch to the app that is required. Let go when you are positioned on the app that you require.

Command-Q

Quit the currently active App.
An alternative way of quitting the app is to click on the App Name in the top menu bar and choose **Quit**

Managing Apps and Windows

Right-click OR click and hold

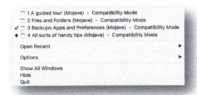

on any open app in the Dock to view a list of the App's open windows (at the top), some options specific to that App, to (in some cases) open a new Window for that app, and to **Quit** the app.

Change order of Apps in Dock by clicking and dragging them to another position.

Some Other Handy App Tips

View all Windows for an App

To quickly see all Windows that you have open for just the current app (called **App Exposé**), tap twice with two fingers on the icon in the Dock, or press Control-▼ (Control and down-arrow). Refer to the guide **A Guided Tour** to discover other ways (Mouse and Trackpad gestures) of invoking the **App Exposé** screen.

Clear the screen of Windows from other apps

To minimise all windows from other Apps that are currently open – and just leave the current App's windows appearing on the screen – press the combination **Command-Option-H**.

Close or Minimize multiple app windows at once

To close or minimise all Windows for the current App, press the **Option** key while clicking Red or Orange lights.

Enlarge screen without hiding dock and menu/status bar

Double-click the top bar (on which the Traffic Lights sit) to enlarge screen to its full height, but not hide the Dock or the Menu/Status bar.

Double-click here again to return to the previous size for the Window.

Managing Apps and Windows

Note. This feature is turned on in **System Settings -> Desktop & dock**, by choosing the **Zoom** option for **Double-click a window's title bar to**.

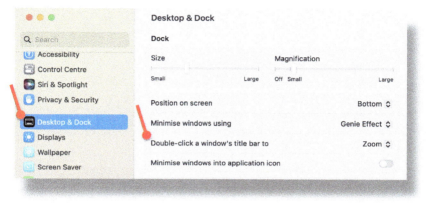

The Standard Apps on your Mac

Your Mac comes with a wealth of standard apps. Here is a brief description of each.

System Settings: As previously mentioned, this is the place to check on and customise the way you want your Mac to operate. It's where you go to setup and define various settings and preferences that apply across you Mac.

Safari: The Safari app is Apple's 'web browser', allowing you to 'surf' the Internet and save bookmarks of favourite sites. This is where you perform your Google searches, look up recipes, research holiday destinations, do your banking online, and so much more! Generally, there is no need for other web browsers like Chrome on your Mac – just use Safari.

Mail: The Mail app gives you easy access to all the email accounts that you use. Various standard functions are provided (Inbox, Sent, Trash, etc.) and, for some types of mail account, you can also set up other mailboxes for filing your mail.

Messages: The Messages App allows you to send Text messages and iMessages, just the same as you do from your iPhone. iMessages are 'internet messages', sent using your iCloud account (which, of course, means your Messages app must be signed in to your iCloud account). Text messages (ie SMS) are only able to be sent as well if your Mac has been set up to interact with your iPhone (which is done from *Settings->Messages->Text Message Forwarding* on your iPhone). Your communications with other people are shown as friendly 'conversations' in speech bubbles.

Contacts: Contacts is your address book on your Mac. It allows you to enter contact information (email address, phone numbers, address – even birthdates) for friends, family, and colleagues. The other Apple Apps on your Mac can then use the information stored in your Contacts to 'auto-fill' people's details when you just enter their name. If you record birthdates of friends and family in your contacts, they will automatically appear in your Calendar and you will be reminded in advance! If your Contacts are stored iCloud or another type of mail account, your Contacts can synchronise between all your devices.

Calendar: Calendar provides you with an electronic diary and calendar. It allows you to set up appointments, engagements and events – and the best thing is that it can provide alerts to remind you about them. If your Calendars are stored iCloud or another type of mail account, your Calendars can synchronise between all your devices.

The Standard Apps on your Mac

Photos: The photos App looks after your photo library. It allows you to view your photos on a timeline, organise pictures into albums, take advantage of facial recognition to identify photos of people, edit, share photos with others, use a photo as your desktop 'wallpaper', and assign photos to people in your address book in the Contacts App. You can run slideshows of your photos or just swipe through full-screen views of your photos. Through iCloud, you can also magically see photos that you have taken on another Apple device! You can also easily import photos from a camera or from your iPad and iPhone, edit photos, and much more.

Music, TV, Podcasts: The Music, TV and Podcasts apps replaced iTunes in macOS Catalina (2019). Music allows you to manage all your music and audio, while TV allows you to manage your movies, TV shows and videos. Podcasts is pretty obvious – it's where you listen to Podasts! While iTunes used to be able to do backups of your iPad & iPhone and syncing of content to these devices, these are now managed from Finder. We won't go into this in detail here (as it is not often used any more), but when you plug your iPhone/iPad into your Mac, the mobile device will appear under Finder's Locations area, with similar options to iTunes.

Notes: This is a wonderfully useful app for recording notes such as shopping lists, keeping a list of books or movies you have been recommended, or just capturing some piece of information that you want to store and access easily. These Notes then synchronise between your Mac and your other Apple devices (if you choose to store your notes in iCloud). More recent versions of the Mac operating system have delivered great enhancements to this app and it now offers a great alternative to using Evernote and OneNote (for those of you who know these apps!). You can now share Notes with others, lock notes, add tags and more.

Maps: Find directions from one place to another by car, foot, or public transportation, view maps, zoom in and out, see places in 3D Satellite view and more. Now you can toss out that street directory.

App Store: As described in Part 1 of our series of guides (called **A Guided Tour**), the Mac App Store allows you to buy and download all sorts of Apps (applications) for your Mac. Mac apps are different to iPad and iPhone apps – so purchasing an app on one of those devices does not usually mean you have access to it on your Mac. It must be separately purchased/downloaded in the majority of cases. App updates are also managed from the App Store. In saying that, the new Macs with M1 chips will be able to run Mac apps 'natively' –

The Standard Apps on your Mac

meaning you won't need to purchase a separate 'Mac' version of the iPad/iPhone App.

FaceTime: The FaceTime app allows you the make a video call to someone who is also on an Apple device. It is similar to Skype and Zoom, and very easy to use. You can also use FaceTime audio – which is like making a phone call without needing a phone!

Photo Booth: This fun app lets you add effects to photos taken using your Mac's camera. The kids love it!

Books: The Books App allows you to buy and download ebooks and audiobooks to read on your Apple devices. It also allows for the saving and storage of PDFs, and the synchronization of books and PDFs to your Apple mobile devices – so that you can easily access them later. Set up Collections to organise your books, add bookmarks and notes, and much more.

Pages, Numbers Keynote: These apps are Apple's equivalent of the Microsoft Office suite of Word, Excel and PowerPoint. **Pages** allows you to create documents, **Numbers** allows creation of spreadsheets, and **Keynote** is for presentations. If you are not particularly skilled in the Microsoft suite, it is worth using this set of **free** Apple apps instead.

iMovie: Become a movie maker, creating movies from clips of videos and photos that you have on your Mac, camera or i-Device. Include fancy transitions, titles, music and more. It's easy and fun.

Preview: A fantastic app that allows for the viewing of PDFs and images, as well as annotating, rearranging, reformatting, and so much more. No need to use Adobe Acrobat Reader or PhotoShop on your Mac – Preview performs so many of the same functions. More about Preview in the fourth part of this **Introduction to the Mac** series of guides.

Quicktime: Plays videos, but also does so much more. More about Quicktime in the fourth part of this **Introduction to the Mac** series of guides.

The Standard Apps on your Mac

Find My: Find My helps you locate and protect your Apple device if it's ever lost or stolen. To use it, you must be signed in to iCloud. When needed, you can use this app to locate your missing device, play a sound (even if it is muted), register it as 'lost' and more. Find My also shows details of any family members and friends who have shared their location with you – allowing you to help locate their devices (and them) as well if needed. If you have accessories like AirTag, you can also track their location and play a sound to locate.

News: The News App was new to the Mac in Mojave and provides the same features as found on the iPad and iPhone version of the app – curated and collated news items from all around the world.

New Apps in macOS Ventura

Clock: The Clock app that we know and love from the iPhone has finally come to the Mac, allowing you to see times in different countries, and set alarms and timers.

Freeform: Also new in Ventura is the Freefrom App, for brainstorming, diagramming, collaborating.

In the next section, we will look at some tips for some of the more frequently used apps.

Some Safari Tips

Safari is the Web Browser built-in to your Mac. It performs the same functions as other Web Browsers - Chrome, Internet Explorer, Mozilla, and Edge. It is the web browser of choice for my Mac, offering great integration with my iOS devices – including a wonderful feature called Continuity, which allows a web page that I am looking at on my iPhone to be immediately viewed on my Mac.

In this guide, we are not aiming to provide a comprehensive lesson on using Safari. Instead, we aim to offer some handy Safari tips to enhance your web browsing on the Mac.

New look 'Start' page in Safari

With the arrival of Big Sur, there were a number of changes to the Safari app.

One of the most noticeable new features is the ability to have a lovely photo as the background for your Start page, the screen that normally appears whenever you request a new Safari page using the + symbol at top right.

This background image can be set up clicking the icon at the bottom right of the screen. The set of options allows you to choose what appears on your Start page).

Some Safari Tips

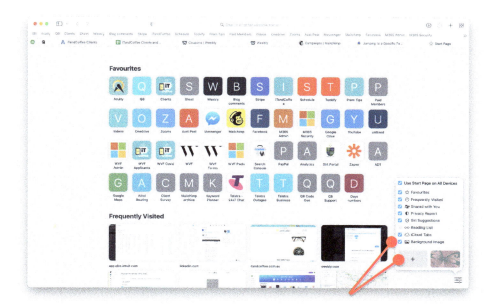

Tick the **Background Image** option, then the + to choose from a range of **Desktop Pictures** – or scroll (swipe right to left) through the patterns provided and choose one of those.

If, when you choose the +, you want to choose a photo from your Photos library (instead of choosing one of Apple's Desktop Pictures), go to the bottom of the left sidebar, to the Media section, and choose Photos. You will then see the content of your Photos library and can make a choice from there.

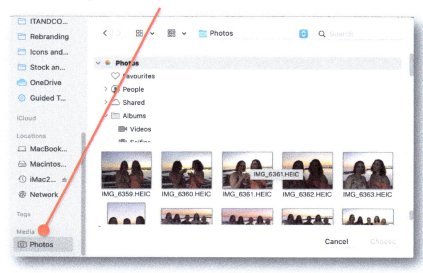

Some Safari Tips

Tab Previews

Also introduced in Big Sur in 2020 were Tab Previews.

If you hover your cursor over any of the Safari 'tabs' shown across the top (which represent the pages that are currently open in your Safari browser), a preview of that page's content appears – allowing you to see what that page contains.

Save 'frequently used' Web pages as Favourites

All web browsers include a feature called 'bookmarking', where it is possible to save/track web pages you may want to refer to later or frequently. You can even put your bookmarks into categories/folders, to list them and organise them. Syncing of these Bookmarks can be handled by iCloud, so that you can see them on all your Apple devices.

There is a special category of Bookmarks, known as your **Favourites.**

Any web pages that you save as your **Favourites** will be shown on the screen that you see when you open a new tab (ie. the Start Page) or click on the search/address bar at the top of the Safari screen.

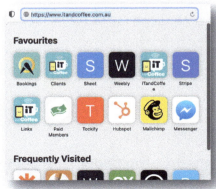

Just click on the applicable icon to open the required page.

Some Safari Tips

Make your Favourites visible all the time in Safari

Clicking on the Search/Address bar in Safari will cause the 'Favourites' pane to appear (as shown in previous image), showing a set of tiles that allow you to choose which of these Favourites you would like to access - or to search for some entirely different web page using the search/address bar.

You can also choose to always show your **Favourites** in a bar that appears below the search field (as indicated above) – making it very easy to get to the pages you use frequently. Just click on the Favourite to go directly to that page.

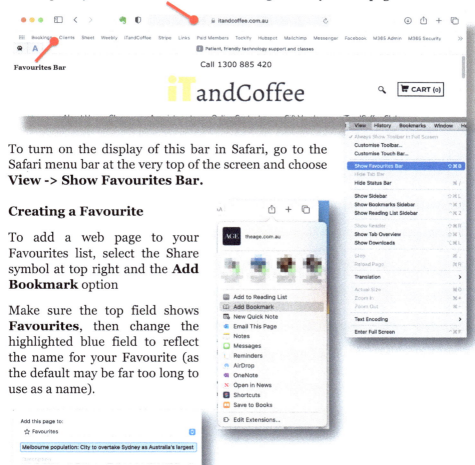

To turn on the display of this bar in Safari, go to the Safari menu bar at the very top of the screen and choose **View -> Show Favourites Bar.**

Creating a Favourite

To add a web page to your Favourites list, select the Share symbol at top right and the **Add Bookmark** option

Make sure the top field shows **Favourites**, then change the highlighted blue field to reflect the name for your Favourite (as the default may be far too long to use as a name).

Your new Favourite will be the last on appearing in the set of tiles and on the Favourites bar.

Some Safari Tips

There is also a quicker way to save a web page as a Favourite.

1. Go to the web page that you want to save.
2. Click in the Search bar. You should see a symbol/icon at the left end – this is called a 'Favicon'.
3. Drag the 'Favicon' for the web page onto the Favourites bar or into the Favourites pane that appears, placing it into the position that you want it to sit.

4. The name of the favourite will be automatically filled in – just rename it to whatever name you choose.
5. To rename it later, right-click on the favourite in the Favourites Bar and choose **Rename.**

Rearranging your Favourites

Just drag the Favourite bookmarks around to re-order them – either on the Favourites Bar or in the pane of tiles.

Removing a Favourite

Just drag the 'Favourite' out of the Favourites bar or the Favourites pane, and it will disappear in a puff of smoke.

Or right-click it in the Favourites Bar (or in the Favourites window below that, if visible) and choose **Remove.**

Reader - Uncluttered viewing of web pages

Safari has a great feature called **Reader**, which allows you to view a web page with just its basic text and images – and without the clutter of advertisements and other extras.

This is great for reading newspaper articles, recipes and more.

Not all web pages will provide you with this option, but it is worth using this feature for any pages that do! Look for pages that have a 'lines' symbol on the left of the Search field.

Some Safari Tips

When you tap the 'lines' symbol, the article/page will come up, stripped of all distractions and in easy-to-read text. In the images below, the left-hand image is the normal web page; right is the **Reader** version.

Reader view can be very handy when you want to send the contents of the web page to someone – or to yourself - via email.

When the page is being viewed in **Reader** format, choosing to mail it to someone will result in an email that contains text and images from the page, without all the ads and other graphics that the page may have. The same applies on an iPad or iPhone.

Just choose the **Share** symbol ⬆ at top right and **Email this Page** to send the web page's Reader format text and images (plus a link to the web page).

Open a new link as a new 'tab' or window

Sometimes it is preferable to ensure that a link opens a new Tab or Window instead of replacing the contents of the current Tab.

Command-click on any link to open the link's web page in a new tab. Or choose **Control-Click** to get the menu of options shown on the right and choose between a New Tab and New Window.

Move a Tab to a new Safari Window

For occasions where it is desirable to view a particular web page at the same time as another web page, it is easy to open a second Safari window from a tab that is already visible.

Some Safari Tips

Simply drag a Safari tab outside the current Safari window to open a separate Safari Window with that Tab.

Or right-click on the tab name and choose **Move Tab to New Window**.

Change the Home Page

If you would like Safari to open with the 'Google' page each time it starts, this can be set up in your **Safari -> Settings**, in the **General** option.

Just set up the first four options to contain the values shown in the image below.

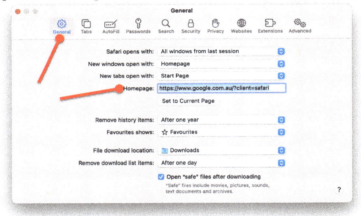

If it is not the Google page you want to see first, simply type the address of your favourite webpage in the **Homepage** field. If you that favourite webpage is the 'current' page, simply choose **Set to Current Page**

Some Navigation Tricks

Click and hold on the < symbol at top left in Safari to see a list of the pages that were visited 'on the way' to the current page.

Click on any of the items in the list to go directly to that page – without having then press < multiple times to get to the page.

Some Safari Tips

After returning to an earlier page, click and hold > to see the list of web pages that you have just left, then click on any item in that list to return to the page.

Save Image from Web Page

Right-click on an image on a web page to save it somewhere.

It can be saved to any folder, or to the Photos app by choosing **Add Image to Photos**.

(Note. Not all images on a web page can be saved – so you may not see this set of options for all of them.)

Zoom in and out

Double-tap with two fingers on the Magic Mouse or Trackpad to quickly zoom in or out. (If this doesn't work, visit **System Settings -> Mouse or System Settings -> Trackpad** to enable this gesture.)

Make Font Bigger and Smaller

Bigger: Command - + (Control combined with Equals/Plus [+] key)

Smaller: Command - – (Control combined with Minus key)

Bookmark Menu

Since macOS Monterey, the Bookmarks icon at the top left (near the 'traffic lights') has provided a different set of options to what previously showed for this option.

This icon controls the sidebar that can appear in Safari, showing Bookmarks, Reading List and History.

Click it once to expose the sidebar, and again to hide the sidebar.

Above left is the look of that sidebar under Catalina. The right shows the look under macOS Ventura.

Some Safari Tips

Previously, the symbols at the top allowed you to choose between viewing your set of Bookmarks, Reading List and History.

These options are now shown at the bottom of the left sidebar.

Tab Groups

A new feature introduced in macOS Monterey in 2021 is one called Tab Groups.

These listings of tabs allow you to organise your frequently used tabs so that you can jump to a listed set really easily. For example, you may have a list of tabs that you use for work and one that you use for home.

You can see and manage your Safari Tab Groups from the sidebar. Click the symbol ▭ to view this sidebar.

When the sidebar is not visible, you will see a 'down-arrow' symbol on the right of the sidebar symbol. ▭ ˅

This provides quick access to your existing set of Tab Groups, and to create new Tab Groups.

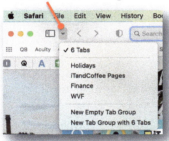

In the screens above, I have set up 4 Tab Groups (Holidays, iTandCoffee Pages, Finance and WVF) – and can quickly switch between my set of tabs and these tab lists – or I can create a new Tab List.

New Tab Groups can be created using the symbol at top right of the sidebar (if it is visible) or by choosing the 'down-arrow' when no sidebar is visible.

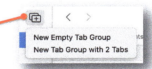

Both these options give **New Empty Tab Group** and **New Tab Group with n Tabs**. The second option will create the Tab Group using the set of tabs that are currently showing in Safari.

Note that Tab Groups are not available from Private Browsing mode.
Learn more about Tab Groups in this Apple Support article:
https://support.apple.com/en-au/guide/safari/ibrwa2d73908/mac

Some Safari Tips

Shared with You

Monterey also brought another option to the Sidebar – the **Shared with You** feature.

Click this option to see all the links that have been shared with you via Messages. This will help you quickly locate such like, without having to trawl through your Messages.

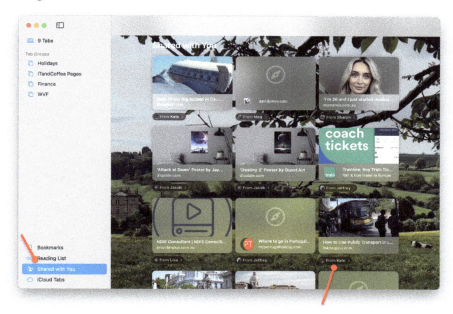

Underneath the thumbnail of each shared link is the name of the person who shared it with you.

New for Safari in macOS Ventura

Many of the new features in Ventura are more advanced features that many users will never utilise. Three relate to Tab Groups – the ability to share Tab Groups with others, set up Tab Groups start pages, pin tabs in a Tab Group.

Website settings will now sync between your Apple devices.

For web pages with images that contain some text, you will be able to use Apple's **Live Text** feature to select and copy text from these images.

To read about the features of macOS Ventura, see Apple's summary at www.apple.com/au/macos/ventura/features.

Some Mail Tips

Introduction

In this section, we cover some handy tips for using Mac's Mail app. These tips are based on the questions we are regularly asked by clients, and highlight features that can really enhance your use of this App. We will not attempt to cover everything there is to know about Mail.

Don't think that you have to use an alternative mail app on the Mac. Your Mail app can handle all of your email accounts in one place, including Gmail, Outlook, Exchange, Yahoo, Hotmail, Bigpond, Optus and more.

Mail can handle multiple email Accounts

As mentioned in the Introduction, your Mail app can manage emails from multiple email accounts. My own Mail apps looks after my iCloud, Gmail, and Exchange email accounts.

To see which email accounts are being managed by your Mail app, go to **Mail -> Settings**, to the **Accounts** option along the top

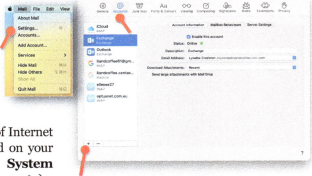

On the left side is the list of Internet Accounts that are installed on your Mac (as also listed in **System Settings -> Internet Accounts**).

For each of these accounts, the right side shows information about the account – including (in the **Account Information** tab along the top) the ability the **Enable this account,** so that it appears in the Mail app, or un-tick to disable the account and not show it in the Mail app. (Note that 'Unticking' this option does not delete any mail data stored for that account. If you re-tick the option, the stored mail will appear again.)

Additional Mail accounts can be added by choosing the + at the bottom of the left sidebar (as indicated above), choosing the type of Mail account you wish to add, then providing the email address & password.

We won't go into detail about adding mail accounts in this guide. If you need assistance with this, iTandCoffee can help.

Some Mail Tips

Nominating the default account for new emails

If you have multiple email accounts – and more than one of those accounts has been 'enabled' in the Accounts option of Mail Settings - it is important to then nominate which account is the 'default' be used when any new email is created, which determines the 'from' email address.

This is achieved in the **Mail -> Settings** (accessed from the top menu bar).

In the **Composing** set of options, look for the **Send new messages from** option, and choose your preferred account from the list provided.

It is important to ensure that all your other devices reflect the same 'default'. On iPad and iPhone, devices, the **Default Account** setting is found towards the end of options in **Settings -> Mail**.

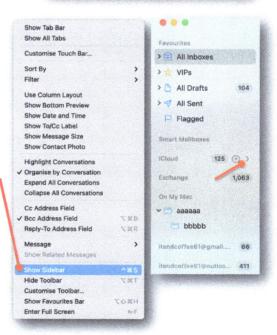

View/hide Mailbox list

If you ever find that you are not able to see the list of mailboxes in the sidebar when viewing the Mail app, it is because your Mailbox list has been 'hidden'.

To show the Mailbox list again, choose **Show Sidebar** from the **View** menu at the top.

Additionally, in the Mailbox list, certain sections may currently be 'hiding' their list of mailboxes.

In the example on the far right, the 'iCloud' list of Mailboxes is hidden. Hover over the word iCloud to see > symbol on right and click this to 'expose' the full Mailbox list under that section.

Same applies if you see > on left side – click this symbol to expand and view any hidden detail. Click the 'down arrow' to hide the detail.

Some Mail Tips

Group mail by conversations

An option that is usually turned on by default is one that groups mail messages by 'Conversation'.

This means that email messages that have the same subject and involve the people from the original message will be grouped, and only the most recent message of the group may appear in the list of mail messages.

A number and double-arrow indicate that there are multiple messages grouped – in the example below right, 9 indicates that there are 9 messages in the conversation.

Clicking on the message or the number that is shown will then reveal the other messages in the 'conversation'.

This grouping can be very handy in some cases, but often means that you have trouble finding emails if you prefer to see messages grouped in order of their date. The required email may be 'hidden' in a conversation.

If you prefer to see all your messages listed without this grouping, untick the **Organise by Conversation** option in the **View** menu.

If you want all the emails in the conversation to be shown in the list of emails (instead of just the most recent), choose **Expand All Conversations** from the **View** menu.

Send Again

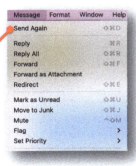

For occasions when you need to re-send an email instead of just 'forwarding' it, go to the Messages menu and choose **Send Again**.

Just change the recipient for this new email.

This is better that forwarding as it doesn't include all the 'forwarding' information that you then need to strip out if you want the message to look like the original.

I use **Send Again** for sending standard emails that I send regularly, emails that I have saved to special Mailboxes as 'templates'.

Some Mail Tips

Choose how to send a Web Page – link, PDF, web page

When choosing to send a Safari web page via email (by choosing the Share symbol and selecting **Email this Page**), you can send the page in one of several different formats in the Mail app.

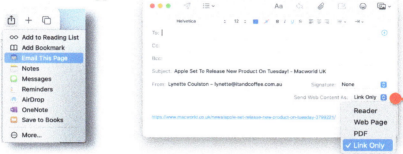

In the draft email window that appears, choose one of the below options in the **Send Web Content As** field (see above right).

The **Reader** option will only be available if the page you are sending is one that supports **Reader** format (which usually only applies to articles). This format will provide the link to the page PLUS the text and images from the article (without any ads and other clutter).

Mail Folders (Mailboxes)

If you have a 'newer' style of email account – an IMAP or Exchange email account – you can choose to organize your mail messages into mail folders, called Mailboxes, in this mail account.

These Mailboxes can then be viewed on any device that manages that mail account.

If you don't have an IMAP or Exchange email account, you can still choose to organize your mail into Mailboxes on your Mac (in which case they won't sync to your other devices).

Mailboxes can be created from the **Mailboxes** menu, by choosing **New Mailbox**.

Choose the **Location** for your new Mailbox by choosing the applicable Mail Account (or choose **On my Mac** if you just want the Mailbox to be stored on the Mac).

Some Mail Tips

Then give your **Mailbox** a name (in the **Name** field).

Nested mailboxes can be created – just choose the 'parent' mailbox in the **Location** field.

Messages can be then dragged and dropped to the mailbox **OR** copied/moved to the mailbox by right-clicking on the message and choosing the applicable action (**Move to** or **Copy to**) and the Mailbox.

An alternative way of creating Mailboxes is to right click hover over the name of the mail account and choose the Plus symbol (+) that appears on the right.

Or right-click on an existing Mailbox and choose the **New Mailbox** option.

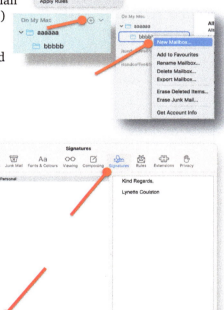

Mail Signatures

A Mail signature is a standard 'sign-off' that appears at the end of every mail message you create. Signatures for your Mail accounts are set up in **Mail -> Settings.** The **Signatures** option appears at top.

To create a mail signature for a Mail account, click on that account in the left-hand frame. Then, choose +.

Click on the default name allocated to the Signature to rename it.

While that new signature is selected in the middle frame, fill in the right-most box with your signature details.

50

Some Mail Tips

Even easier, create a signature in a draft email – with the text sizing and colours, and perhaps an image, and then copy and paste that signature into the box.

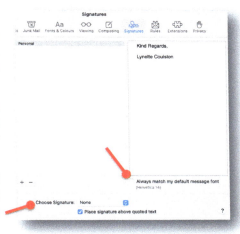

Before you paste in the signature though, **untick the box** underneath that area of the screen – the **Always match my default message font** checkbox.

Having created your signature, you need to now set it as the signature that should show whenever you create an email for that account.

click the **Choose Signature** field towards the bottom of the window and choose the name of the signature that you just created.

You may find that when you click the **Choose Signatures** arrows, there are no options available other than None.

Click on **All Signatures** at top of the left sidebar, then click on the applicable mail account again. The **Choose Signature** field should then allow you to choose the new signature.

Next time you create an email for that mail account, your signature will be added to the mail message.

If you would like to use that same signature for another email account, simply drag that signature from the middle pane to on top of the applicable email account in the left pane.

This will add the signature to that account as well. Then, go to the **Choose Signature** field for that mail account to choose that signature as the default signature for all new emails for that email account.

Selecting and working with multiple messages

When working with mail messages, it is often necessary to perform an action on many messages at once – for example to delete several messages at once, or to move a set of messages to a Mailbox.

When it comes to selecting multiple Mail messages, the same principles apply as described in the **Files, Folders and Finder** guide.

Some Mail Tips

Selecting multiple messages – consecutive messages in list

- Click the first message to select it.
- Move the cursor to the last message that you wish to select.
- Before clicking that last message, **HOLD DOWN THE SHIFT KEY** and click this last message while this shift key is being held down.
- This will then show all the selected messages highlighted in blue.

Selecting multiple messages – random selection

Sometimes the messages that need to be put into a mailbox or need to be deleted are not appearing consecutively in the list of messages.

In this case, **hold down the Command key as you click each message**.

This will allow your message selection to be random.

Click a selected message a second time to 'unselect' it.

Selecting All messages

Command-A will select all messages that are in the current view.

If you require most of the messages in the current view with some exceptions, choose **Command-A** to select all, then hold the Command key and click (to unselect) any items that you want to exclude from the selection.

Then choose what to do with the selection

Having selected a set of mail messages, you may want to then

- **Delete** them – by pressing the **delete** key on the keyboard or the 'trash can' in the top toolbar
- **Move** or **Copy** them to a Mailbox – by dragging them to the Mailbox or choosing Move or Copy from the right-click menu.
- **Mark** them as Read or Flag them (use right-click to find these options)
- Or any other action that might apply to multiple messages.

Some Mail Tips

Searching email

If your Inbox is anything like mine, it can be difficult to keep your incoming mail under control. Finding a message in the long list of emails can be tricky.

A feature that I use multiple times every day is that which allows me to search for a mail message in the current mailbox, or across all mailboxes – based on the sender, subject, content and various other search criteria. This is done using the Search field - the magnifying glass at top right.

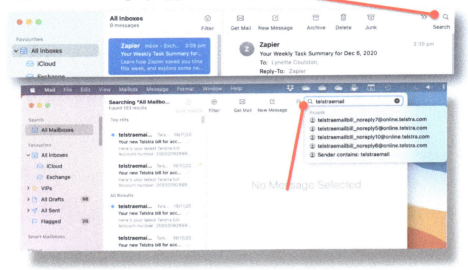

Just start typing the search phrase in the **Search** box at top right.

Suggestions appear below. If you see one that matches what you seek, click it. Otherwise, just hit **return/enter** to see all emails that match the search phrase.

The **sidebar on the left** then changes slightly, to include a new item at the top – **All Mailboxes**. (This was a change introduced in Big Sur – and replaced the bar that used to appear along the top.)

The purpose of this is to allow you to **choose the 'Search Domain'** for your search. If you wish to search across all of your Mailboxes, click **All Mailboxes**.

If you wish to search a specific mailbox, select that mailbox from the list in the sidebar. The results that you see will change based on that selection.

When you have finished your search, click the ⓧ on the right of the search field.

It is important that you clear any search value to return to your 'unfiltered' view of your mail messages.

Some Mail Tips

View and use 'Previous Recipients'

The Mail app has a clever feature that ensures that it 'remembers' the details of those with whom you communicate via email.

Many people assume that, because the Mac seems to 'remember' these email addresses, that these details must automatically be recorded in **Contacts**.

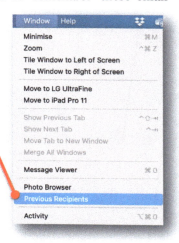

This is not the case – this information is not 'permanently' saved unless you specifically choose to store it in the Contacts app.

The good news is that it is easy to quickly add the details of those with whom you communicate to the Contacts app.

Simply go to the **Window** menu of Mail (in the menu bar) and choose **Previous Recipients.**

Previous Recipients shows a list of all people with whom you have communicated using email, along with the email address that was applicable.

This is the place that you can remove an incorrect or old email address so that it doesn't appear again when you are drafting an email. Simply click on that redundant email address in the list and choose **Remove from List.**

Those 'recipients' who are in your Contacts will have a small 'contact' symbol on the right of the name.

Any that don't have this symbol are not yet in your contacts.

Select individual items and choose the **Add to Contacts** option, or use the technique described for selecting several items from the list (using the Shift or Command keys), then choose **Add to Contacts** for that selection.

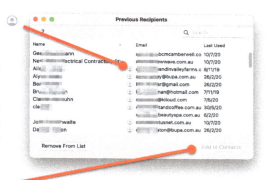

Some Mail Tips

Add mail senders/receivers to Contacts

The other quick way to add someone in your **Mail** app to the **Contacts** app is to click on the 'down-arrow' that appears to the right of the 'From' or 'To' name in the message, to see a list of options for what to do with that sender/recipient.

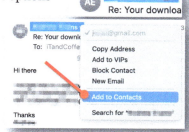

Choose **Add to Contacts** (which will only appear if the email address is not already in your Contacts) to add that email address as a new Contact. In most cases, this will add the Contact correctly with the First and Last names and the email address automatically filled in.

In some cases, however, you may then need to go to the Contact Card and correct or add details.

Click on the down-arrow again and choose **Show Contact Card**, then choose the **Open with Contacts** option at the top right. Then, in the Contacts app, choose **Edit** to modify the details of that contact.

Choosing that down-arrow next to a sender or recipient may also give you the **Remove from Previous Recipients List** option. Choose this to stop that email address coming up when starting to type a name in the 'To', 'Cc' or 'Bcc' field.

Mailing a 'list'

In the next section we will look at how to create a **List** (i.e. group) of **Contacts**.

But how do you go about emailing that List? We will also cover this in the next section, showing the options available for selecting this list when creating an email.

Some Mail Tips

Set up Smart Mailboxes

Just as your Finder provides you with the option of setting up **Smart Folders** (whereby the content of the folder is automatically populated based on a set of Rules), the same thing is possible in your Mail App – by setting up a **Smart Mailbox**.

For example, you may wish your **Smart Mailbox** to show all mail received from a certain set of Contacts; or you may to wish to set up a Smart Mailbox that shows all the mail that has been 'flagged' with a particular colour.

To set up a Smart Mailbox, choose **Mailbox –> New Smart Mailbox** (from the menu bar). Then, give the Smart Mailbox a name and fill in the rules that will apply to that Mailbox.

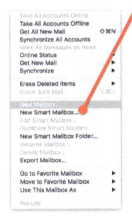

When you choose **OK**, your new Smart Mailbox will be magically populated with all the emails that meet the nominated criteria.

Smart Mailboxes are shown in a section called **Smart Mailboxes** in your Mailbox list and are indicated by a 'wheel' on the left.

If this list is not visible, hover the mouse over the words **Smart Mailboxes** and click > to expand the list.

List of new Mail features in macOS Ventura

A range of new features arrived for Mail in late 2022, including:
- Schedule an email
- Set a reminder for a mail message
- Recall an email within 10-30 secs of send
- Warn of forgotten attachment
- Rich Links (Link Previews)
- Follow Up feature for sent emails needing response
- Notification if recipient missing

Some Mail Tips

We won't attempt to cover all of these in detail in this guide, but here is a bit more information about some of them.

Schedule Send (macOS Ventura)

A new feature delivered as part of macOS Ventura in late 2022 is the ability to defer sending of an email until a later time. Simply click on the down-arrow on right of the Send symbol ⊿ to choose one of the options provided – or choose **Send Later...** to choose a custom time.

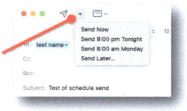

Undo Send (macOS Ventura)

If you realise you have made an error immediately after sending an email, you can now 'Undo Send' to retrieve that email – but you must do so within 30 seconds (or less, depending on your settings).

After an email is sent, the **Undo Send** option will appear at the bottom of the left sidebar

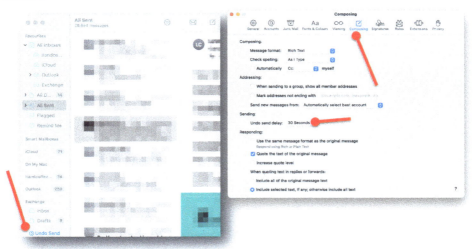

The 'send delay' duration can be customised from **Mail->Settings**, from the Composing section. Choose between 10 and 30 seconds - or turn off the delay completely if you don't want to utilise it.

Some Mail Tips

Remind yourself about an email (macOS Ventura)

macOS Ventura includes the capability to set a reminder for an email in your Inbox, so that you get an alert at a nominated time – to remind you to do something with that email.

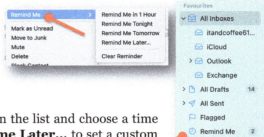

Right-click on an Inbox message in the list and choose a time for your reminder – or **Remind me Later...** to set a custom time/date.

The message will then show a clock on the right side, to indicate a reminder has been set and will appear under a special new Smart Mailbox – the **Remind Me** mailbox.

An alert will appear at top right (assuming your Notifications for Mail are turned on in **System Settings -> Notifications**) when at the nominated time – click on that notification to jump to the email.

Once the alert has appeared, the message will show **REMIND ME** at top right

To set a new time for the reminder, click on the email and choose **Edit** at top right.

To clear the 'remind me', right-click on the message preview and choose **Remind Me,** then **Clear Reminder**.

If you want to see all the emails for which reminders have been set (including those with an expired reminder date/time), the best way to do this is to sort your inbox by **Remind Me**.

This is done from the **View** menu's **Sort By** option, by choosing **Remind Me**.

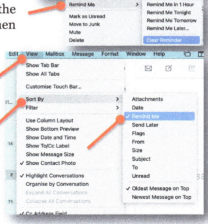

Some Mail Tips

Missing Attachments (macOS Ventura)

If you draft an email that mentions inclusion of an attachment, but that then doesn't include such an attachment, you will get a warning under macOS Ventura.

I found that this new feature depended very much on the wording of the message and/or subject. For some messages that mention something like 'attached is the requested file', I did not get any such warning.

Hopefully this feature will improve over time.

Sending links with a 'preview' (macOS Ventura)

If you send a link as part of an email, you can now choose to send it as a 'friendly' looking attachment, as shown in the image on the right.

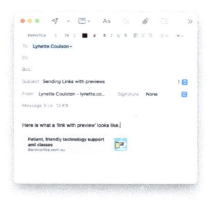

To generate this 'look' for the link, type (or paste) the URL. You will see a down-arrow appear on the right of the text, when your mouse pointer is positioned on or near the address.

Click that down-arrow and choose **Show Link Preview**.

Follow Up (macOS Ventura)

The new Follow Up feature of macOS Ventura seems to have limited value right now. The idea of it is that, if the Mail app detects that you haven't received a reply from someone after a period of time (not sure what that time period is!), you may see the message that you sent appear magically at the top of your Inbox – to remind you to follow up with that person.

I think it depends on the content of the message you send. You don't have any control over this, which makes its value very limited. We won't go into this feature further as part of this guide – and will hope that it improves over time.

Some Contacts Tips

Introduction

In this section, we cover some handy tips for using Mac's Contacts app. The **Contacts** app is your Address Book for Mac, and corresponds with the same app on the iPhone and iPad

The information stored in **Contacts** is used by many applications on Mac – **Calendar**, **Mail, Messages**, **Phone**, **Facetime**, **Maps**, and more.

By ensuring that the details of the people that you contact and visit are entered and maintained in this digital address book, you will find it so much easier to keep in touch with them using your Mac.

By 'syncing' your Contacts using iCloud, Gmail, Outlook, Yahoo, Exchange or any other IMAP email account, any contacts you add or change on your computer will automatically be added/updated on your other devices (provided that they are all associated with the same IMAP/Exchange account).

Contact Groups become Lists (macOS Ventura)

Do you have a group of people who you need to email on a regular basis?

This could be your team, committee members, your book group, your family, or just a list of friends.

Under macOS Ventura, such a group is known as a **List**. Prior to macOS Ventura, the term was used by Apple was Group.

Create Contact Lists

Creation of **Contact Lists** is done in the **Contacts** App. The process is

- Create your Contact List
- Then drag Contacts into this List

Contacts are not 'moved' to the list - the **Contact List** is simply a listing or index of contacts that exist in the main list and a single Contact can appear in multiple Lists.

First make sure your 'Lists' are visible

Before creating the List, check that you are seeing a list of your existing 'Lists' in the sidebar on the left of your Contacts app.

To make the 'Lists' sidebar appear, go to the **View** menu and choose **Show Lists**

Some Contacts Tips

Now create the List

Now you are ready to create your list.

1. Just click on the + symbol, at the bottom of the right-hand pane.

2. You will see a list of options. Choose **New List.**

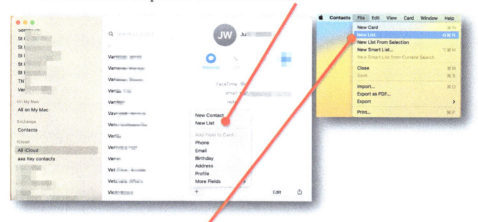

3. Or choose **File->New List**

4. A new List will appear in your list of Lists, with the name **untitled list** – which can be replaced with the list's name immediately, while it is in this 'edit mode' (highlighted in blue).

> untitled list

5. If it is not selected/highlighted as shown above, simply click this new list to select it, then click again to edit the default name.

6. Then, find the contacts that belong in this list and drag them on top of the new list's name.

7. Voila - you have created your list! The example on right shows my **Family** list which includes my husband and kids and partners.

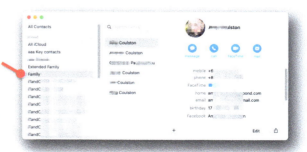

Keep in mind that, even though you might add people to this list, to email these people as a list, you will need to ensure that each Contact Card has an email address.

Some Contacts Tips

Some Contacts Tips

Now it's time to email that list

Emailing a list is very easy and can be achieved in a few different ways.

Option 1. From Contacts, right-click on the list and choose **Send Email to *list-name*.** The Mail app will appear, with a New Message containing the list members in the 'To' field.

Option 2. In the Mail app, start a new message, then start typing the name of the List, and it will appear in the list of Contacts. Just tap the List's name to select it and see all the members' email addresses appear in the 'To' field.

In the example below, the list I am emailing is **Family**, so I have typed 'family' and can then click on that item in the list that appears below.

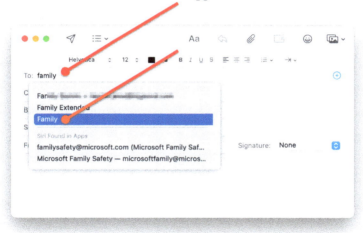

Option 3: If you have the **Contacts** app visible when you create the new email, just drag the List from the Contacts sidebar into the 'To' (or 'Cc' or 'Bcc') field of your email. All of the list members' email addresses will appear.

Some Contacts Tips

Show the List Name (not members) in Mail's To, Cc

It is possible to just show the List Name in the 'To' field, instead of the full list of contacts that are in the list.

This is a Setting in the __Mail__ app.

Go to **Mail -> Settings -> Composing**.

Un-tick the **When sending to a group ...** option indicated in the above left image. (It seems that, at the time of writing this book, they have not yet changed that option to refer to a 'list'!)

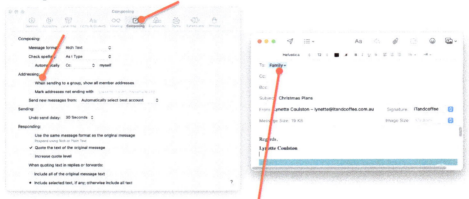

Then, you will see just the name of the list – as shown above right.

Note. Those receiving the email will still see the full list of recipients – not just the list name – if they are not Apple Mail users (unless you use the bcc field to hide the recipient list).

Resolve Duplicate Contacts

It can be quite easy to end up with duplicated contacts in the **Contacts** app.

Luckily, it is very easy to clean up and merge duplicated contacts.

In the Contacts app, just select **Card -> Look for Duplicates** (from the Menu Bar at the top).

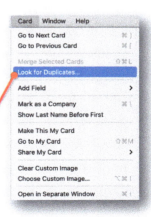

Some Contacts Tips

Choose **Merge** to sort out the duplicated information.

You may need to, in some cases, make a choice on which contact to use – or whether to keep both.

In cases where you have two (or more) Contact Cards that are actually the same person, select those Contact Cards and choose **Card -> Merge and Link Selected Cards.**

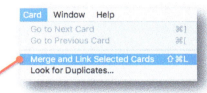

Save contacts from other sources

In the previous section we looked at how to save Contacts from the Mail App.

The same method of saving contact details applies to the Messages and Facetime apps.

Just click on the 'down-arrow' at the side of the of the 'From' contact and choose **Create New Contact** or **Add to Existing Contact.**

Share Contact Cards (but not everything)

It is easy to Share a contact with someone else – ie to send the details of that Contact via email or text.

When sharing a Contact with another person, it is important to consider whether you wish to send the person's photo and any Notes you have recorded as well – especially if you have recorded any information that you may consider 'private'.

In **Contacts->Settings->vCard** (at top right), un-tick

- **Export notes in vCard's** and
- **Export photos in vCard's**

if you don't wish to include these details when sharing a Contact Card with someone else.

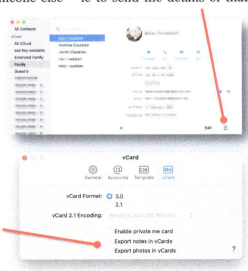

Some Contacts Tips

Order of display of Contacts

As with other Apps, the preferences and settings for **Contacts** can be found in the top menu bar, in **Contacts -> Settings**.

A couple of key Settings that you may wish to adjust in the **General** area of Contacts Settings are:

- **Show First Name**

- **Sort By**

I prefer to **Show First Name** *Before last name*, and the **Sort By** *first name*.

Contacts can come from multiple accounts

In the next section we will talk about Calendars and, in particular, the fact that Calendars are linked to your Mail accounts/s. The same applies for Contacts – Contacts are (generally) associated with a mail account.

To see which email accounts are showing their Contacts in the Contacts app, look at the **Accounts** option in **Contacts -> Settings**.

On the left side is the list of Internet Accounts that are installed on your Mac (as listed in **System Settings -> Internet Accounts**).

For each of these accounts, the right side shows information about the account – including the ability the **Enable this account**, or un-tick to disable the account (and not show it in the Contacts app).

Some Contacts Tips

Nominating the default account for new Contacts

If you have multiple email accounts – and more than one of those accounts has been 'enabled' in the Accounts option of Contacts - it is important to then nominate which account is the 'default' be used when any new Contact card is created – i.e. where new Contacts should be stored.

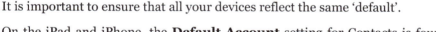

This is achieved in **Contacts -> Settings** (accessed from the top menu bar).

In the **General** set of options, look for the **Default Account** option, and choose your preferred account– in the example shown here, my 'iCloud' account is my default.

It is important to ensure that all your devices reflect the same 'default'.

On the iPad and iPhone, the **Default Account** setting for Contacts is found in **Settings -> Contacts**.

Some Calendar Tips

Introduction

In this section, we cover some handy tips for using Mac's Calendar app. The **Calendar** app is your diary/planner for Mac, and corresponds with the same app on the iPhone and iPad

By ensuring that that all your events – appointments, meetings, dinners, lunches, etc – are added to your Calendar, your Mac (and, usually, your iPad and iPhone) can keep you informed of what you have on each day and notify you of upcoming events in the hour or two beforehand (you choose when).

By 'syncing' your Calendar using iCloud, Gmail, Outlook, Yahoo, Exchange or any other 'IMAP' email account, any calendar events you add or change on your computer will automatically be added/updated on your other devices (provided that they are all associated with the same IMAP/Exchange account).

A similar look to the iPad

The Calendar App on the Mac looks very similar to that which appears on the iPad.

Along the top are the options to choose a **Day, Week, Month or Year** view. Also available is the **Today** option, to take you straight to today's date.

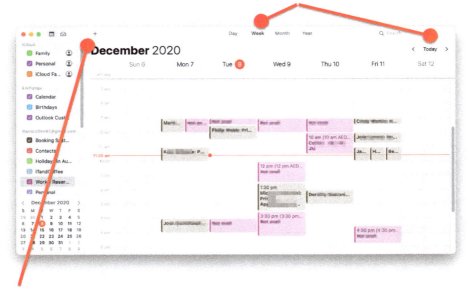

+ allows for the addition of a new event. Even better, double-click on any spot on the calendar to create an event.

Some Calendar Tips

Show list of Calendars

In the example shown above, the option **Show Calendar List** has been selected from the **View** menu, so that all the available calendars are in view in the left sidebar.

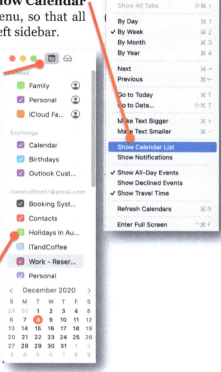

Alternatively, click the **Calendar** symbol at top left (next to the traffic lights) to hide or display this list of Calendars.

Turning Calendars on and Off

Tick and un-tick individual calendars in the Calendars sidebar to show or hide their events on the calendar screen.

If you find that a set of events is missing from your Calendar, it may simply be that the corresponding calendar has been inadvertently 'un-ticked'.

Calendars can come from multiple accounts

Where do your 'Calendars' come from?

Calendars are linked to your Mail or iCloud account - so you may find that you have calendars from more than one account.

You can also have a calendar that appears only on your Mac and is not linked to any mail account.

Account-based Calendars are enabled or disabled in **Internet Accounts**, in **System Settings.**

For those Internet Accounts that are capable of having a Calendar associated with them, just tick this feature to in **System Settings -> Internet Accounts** to activate it on your Mac and show that account's Calendar/s in the Calendar app. Alternatively, untick the Calendar

Some Calendar Tips

feature on any Internet Accounts that you don't wish to appear in the Calendars app.

The list of **Accounts** used by the Calendar app can also be managed from **Calendar -> Settings.**

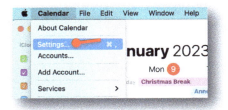

Click the **Accounts** section heading (along top), then click the relevant account on the left. Ensure the **Enable this account** box is ticked if you want the account's calendar to be visible in the **Calendar** app.

Create a new Calendar

In addition to the setting up of Calendars from multiple accounts, it is also possible to set up multiple calendars in the same account, to cover the different parts of your life.

To create a new calendar, choose **File -> New Calendar**.

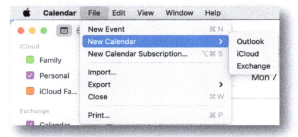

If you have enabled Calendars from more than one account, also choose the Account in which the new Calendar should be created.

A new 'Untitled' calendar will appear in the list – simply re-name it as required.

Some Calendar Tips

Change the Calendar's Colour or Name

Different colours can be used for your different calendars – either from the same account, or from different accounts.

To set up the colour of your Calendar, right-click its name in the **Calendars** list in the sidebar and choose the colour from the standard set provided (or Custom Colour to choose an alternative colour).

Choose the **Get Info** option to see other details of the Calendar. This is alternative place where you can change the name of the calendar. (You can also just click a second time on the Calendar's name in the sidebar to edit it.)

Changing the Calendar for an event

Choosing the event's calendar can be done when the event is created or at a later time

In the example on the right, I simply double-clicked on the box representing the 12:30pm timeslot and was given the right-hand form to fill in (with the name of the event and, if required, other details).

At the top right of that form is a coloured box representing my default calendar (which we will discuss soon).

By clicking on the arrow on right of this box, I can choose an alternative calendar for this event.

After the event has been created, its Calendar can be easily changed by right-clicking the event and hovering the mouse over the **Calendar** option, then choosing from the list of available Calendars that appear.

Some Calendar Tips

Nominating the default calendar for new events

If you have multiple Calendars in your Calendar app, it is important to nominate which Calendar is the 'default' calendar to be used when any new event is created.

This is achieved in the **Calendar -> Settings** (accessed from the top menu bar).

In the **General** set of options, look for the **Default Calendar** option, and choose your preferred Calendar – in the example shown on the right, my 'Work – Reserved' calendar is my default.

Sharing Calendars

iCloud Calendars are able to be shared with one or more other iCloud users – providing a great way of ensuring that members of the family are aware of events that impact them.

Shared Calendars are indicated by a ⓐ symbol on the right-hand side.

Sharing is set up by right-clicking on the calendar name and choosing **Share Calendar...**

Enter the **iCloud/Apple ID** of the other person in the **Share With...** field.

You can only share with another iCloud user.

Once sharing has been set up, it can be modified by right-clicking on the calendar name and choosing **Sharing Settings** or **Stop Sharing**.

Some Calendar Tips

Recurring events

If you have an event that occurs on a regular basis – for example, an exercise class every week – such events can be set up as Recurring events.

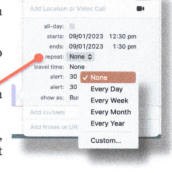

When creating or editing the event click on the date to expand out the options associated with this event.

The **repeat** option will become available. Click on this to uncover your 'repeat' options (right).

The **Custom** option provides a great set of choices, including the ability to specify something like 'last Tuesday of every month'.

Having chosen how often the event repeats, the choice can then be made on when the event ends.

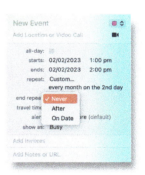

Choose the **end repeat** option (if applicable) to set this up, then choose whether to end on a specific date, or after a certain number of repeats.

Setting Default Alert Times

You can set up standard alert times (e.g. 30 minutes before, one day before) for different 'types' of calendar event, to ensure you receive a reminder (with sound) about the event.

It is a good idea to set up this default, so that you don't have to remember to choose an **Alert** timeframe every time you create an event.

1. Go to **Calendar -> Settings**, to the **Alerts** option.

2. Define default alerts for each type of event: Event, All-Day Events and for Birthdays (more later).

Some Calendar Tips

3. You can also click the **Time to leave** option which, if you have put full location information into your event, will warn you when it is time to leave, based on current traffic conditions. (The Location of the event must be a valid address known to Maps.)

Birthdays in the Calendar

You may or may not have noticed that there is a special 'calendar' that Apple provides for you – one that shows your birthdays and anniversaries.

Birthday and anniversary information can magically appear in your Calendar based on information you have stored about your friends and family in **Contacts**.

Birthday events have a little 'gift box' on their left and are shown as 'all-day' events.

For important people in your life, it is a good idea to add their birthdays to the Contact card you have created for them in the Contacts app. You will find the **Birthday** field immediately after the 'Address' field.

I don't see any birthdays in my Calendar!

If you have set up some birthdays in your Contacts, but still don't see these birthdays in your Calendar, it is probably because your 'Birthdays' calendar is not enabled.

Go to your Calendars list (sidebar) and make sure Birthdays is ticked in the section titled **Other.**

Note that Mail accounts other than iCloud can also provide Birthday calendars. So if you don't use iCloud for your Contacts, look for a Birthdays calendar under you alternative account.

A quick look at the Notes App

Over recent years, Apple has made lots of enhancements to the Notes app, so that it is now an incredibly useful app – one that I use every day.

This app can hold all sorts of information – 'to do' lists, a set of photos or scans, curated articles, recipes, PDF documents, hand-drawn notes, tables of information – anything really.

The Notes can be organised into folders and sub-folders – making it easier to find the note you need. And there are advanced search capabilities that can even find words within images and scans.

Using iCloud, your Notes can synchronise between all your Apple devices – which means you have access to all your Notes on the go!

So let's look at some key features of the Notes app.

Name your Notes

Notes are created by choosing the Compose Note symbol in the top toolbar.

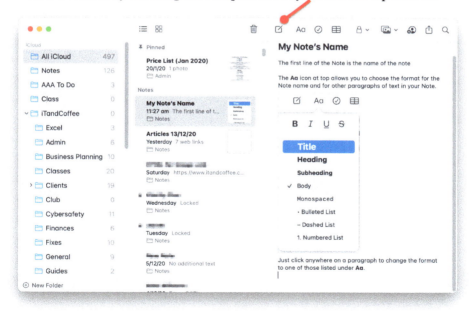

The first line of your Note is the name of the note – the title that will appear in the index listing your notes.

Make this name meaningful, so that you can easily find your Note later.

A quick look at the Notes App

Organise Notes into folders and sub-folders for easier access

Set up as many folders and sub-folders as you need, to organise/group your Notes.

There are a couple of ways to do this. One is to right-click on a folder in the left sidebar and choose **New Folder**.

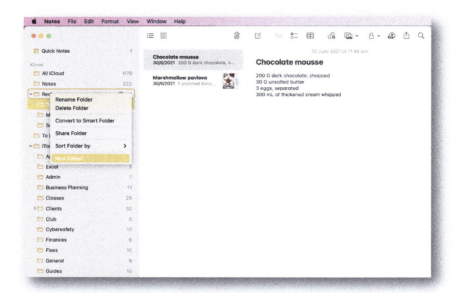

All iCloud is a special folder that shows all notes, no matter what folder they 'live' in.

If you right-click on **All iCloud** and choose **New Folder**, the folder will be created as a 'top' level folder.

If the New Folder is created by right-clicking on a folder underneath All iCloud, then you are creating a sub-folder of that folder.

There is also the **New Folder** option in the File menu.

As with the Finder app, a > symbol appears on the left of a folder name when the content of the folder is hidden. Click that symbol to see the list of sub-folders. Click again to hide the sub-folders.

A quick look at the Notes App

I don't see the All iCloud folder

If you don't see **All iCloud**, it means you have not enabled Notes in your iCloud settings, in -> **System Settings** -> **Apple ID** -> **iCloud** (or it could be you are not signed in to iCloud).

It is a good idea to store your Notes in iCloud, so that they are sync'd to your other Apple devices - and so that Notes you create/change on those other devices are also shown on your Mac. iCloud Notes also give you more features than Notes stored with, say, your Gmail or Outlook account.

Re-organising / Re-ordering Notes folders

Folders can be re-arranged and re-organised by dragging them on top of another folder (to become a sub-folder of that folder) or by dragging to a new position in the list.

Right-click on any folder to choose the automatic sort order for the items in that folder.

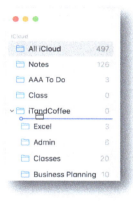

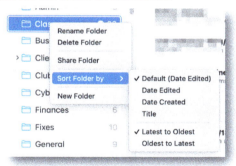

Pin Important Notes to the top of the list

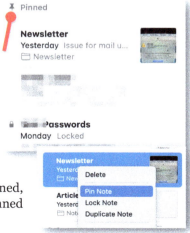

If you have a Note that you want to ensure is always front and centre at the top of the list, you can choose to 'Pin' that Note to the top.

As shown in the image on right, there will then be a **Pinned** section at the top for these Pinned Notes.

To **Pin** a Note to the top, just right-click on the note in Notes list and choose **Pin Note**; once Pinned, choose **Unpin Note** to remove it from the Pinned list.

A quick look at the Notes App

Lock Notes to protect the content

A fantastic feature of Notes on all Apple devices is the ability to Lock any notes that contain sensitive information – such as passwords, account numbers, a perhaps a scanned image of your driver's license or passport.

This is done by right-clicking on the Note in the list and choosing **Lock Note** (refer image on right) or selecting the Note (so it appears on the right of screen) and clicking the 'lock' symbol in the bar at the top and the **Lock Note** option

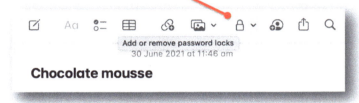

There will be a single Password that will apply for any Notes that you lock, and this same Password will apply to Notes across all the devices associated with the same iCloud account. The first time you lock a Note, you will be asked to set this password. You will also then be given the option to use Face ID or Touch ID to unlock your locked Notes – to save you keying your password every time you want to access a locked Note. Alternatively, you can set up and manage this password and its settings from **Notes -> Settings**.

Lock Note using Custom Password OR Mac's Password (macOS Ventura)

The Lock Notes feature has, up until Ventura, required setting of a separate passcode that then applies across your Locked Notes.

In macOS Ventura the option has been provided in **Notes -> Settings** to **Use Custom Password** or **Use Login Password** when a Note is locked.

If you choose the **Use Custom Password** option, the Password can be anything you choose - all numbers, all letters, or can be a combination of numbers, letters, symbols.

A quick look at the Notes App

Custom Password MUST be remembered

Very Important: The key thing when setting this Custom Password is that **it must be remembered forever** if you want to be able to continue to access the Notes locked with that password.

This applies even if you choose to enable unlocking by Face ID or Touch ID.

The password will still be required at some point in future - for example, when you set up a new device, you will need to enter the password before you can enable Touch ID or Face ID for that Notes on that device.

The password cannot be recovered if you forget it.

You can reset this Custom Password for future Notes, but past Notes that were previously locked with the forgotten password will remain inaccessible without that password.

If you *do* forget the password – but are lucky enough to still have access to the locked Note using Touch ID or Face ID on another device - you do have a 'get out of jail!

On the device that can still access a Locked Note, simple open it with Touch ID or Face ID and **Unlock it.**

This is done using the Share symbol and choosing **Remove Lock** from the Share menu.

Do this for <u>every</u> locked Note, so that no locks remain. Then you can set a new Password from **Notes -> Settings** (in the menu bar at top).

I love Checklists

Choose the Checklist symbol at the top to start a checklist at the current cursor position.

A circle is provided on the left of each item – click this circle to 'tick off' the item in the list.

If you would like newly ticked items to automatically jump to the end of the list, go to **Notes -> Settings** and tick the option labelled **Automatically sort ticked items**.

You can also now indent items in the list so that they become 'sub-items' of the previous item.

A quick look at the Notes App

Use the **tab** key to indent a Note to make it subordinate to the Note above.

To remove this indenting, choose **shift-tab**

Scan directly into Notes

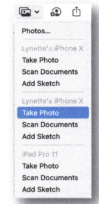

The 'picture' icon along the top provides the option to take a photo or scan a document directly into your Note using your iPhone.

From the picture symbol in the top bar, choose the Take Photo or Scan Documents option, then go to your phone to complete the required action.

You can even sketch something on your iPad – perhaps using your Apple Pencil – straight into the Note on your Mac!

Create/edit Notes from iCloud.com

Even when you don't have your iPhone, iPad or Mac, you can always access and edit your Notes using your web browser.

Visit iCloud.com and sign in with your iCloud Apple ID and password. You will then see a screen with various Apple apps, reflecting the data that you can manage via iCloud.com.

The Notes option gives a web page that looks very similar to your Notes app on your Mac and provides many (but not all) of the capabilities of Notes on your other devices.

A quick look at the Notes App

Sharing Notes (changes in macOS Ventura)

This is one that I use regularly. If you have a Note that another person needs to be able to see and perhaps update, you can Share a Note.

The way in which you Share Notes has changed in macOS Ventura.

To Share a Note that you are currently accessing in Notes, choose the Share symbol at top right (or right-click on a Note in the list and choose **Share Note**).

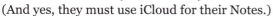

A Note can be shared in two ways – as a **Copy** (where a copy of the Note is sent, usually via Mail, Messages, or Airdrop) or to **Collaborate** with other iCloud users (one or more) (And yes, they must use iCloud for their Notes.)

For **Collaborate**, always consider the 'access permissions' that should apply for the collaboration – click on the **only invited people can edit** text (which appears under the Collaborate option) to expand and see your options, as shown on the right. Choose

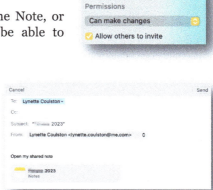

- if those you share with should only be able to view the Note or if they can edit it
- if you anyone with the link to access the Note, or whether only specific invitees should be able to access it.
- If you want those you share with to be able to invite others to share the note.

Then choose how you wish to send the 'Share' invitation Note. The image on the right shows what the draft email looks like when Mail is chosen.

A note that has been Shared will have a little ⊙ icon on the left in the preview list and will show the 👥 symbol toward top right when it is selected as the active Note.

A quick look at the Notes App

Click the  symbol to

- see the **Latest Updates** from participants
- **message** those you have shared with
- **Show All Activity** to see who has made what changes and when (see image far right)
- **Manage Shared Note** (see image on right) to view the list of Participants, share with more people, change permissions, copy the 'share link', Stop Sharing, and more.
- **Show Highlights** to see your Note annotated with the changes that each person made and when (see example below of a shared note relating to a group holiday).

If your Note has been shared with full permissions, you will find that, if you are in the Note at the same time as the other person and that person makes changes, you will see the changes they make occurring before your eyes!

A great example of where this can come in handy is a grocery list that is shared with all household members, so that everyone can contribute to the list.

Important Note. Locked Notes cannot be shared.

Share a whole folder

Sometimes it is not just a single Note that you wish to share. You may wish to share an entire Folder and its Notes.

To share a Folder, simply right-click on the folder and choose **Share Folder**. (Note that a folder can only be shared if it does not contain any Locked Notes.)

A quick look at the Notes App

Mentions for Shared Notes

In macOS Monterey, Apple introduced the capability the 'mention' a person in your Shared Note (must be one of the people with whom you have shared), and they will get a notification that they have been mentioned – and will then be able to jump directly to their 'mention' in the Shared Note.

All you have to do is type an @ symbol and the list of people sharing the Note will appear. Select the person you wish to Mention (see image above right).

Mentions show in blue text in your Note.

When someone mentions you in a text, you will receive a Notification on your Apple devices (assuming Notes is allowed to notify you), advising that you have been mentioned in a Note.

Note Tags

A feature that arrived as part of macOS Monterey in 2021 is Tags. A tag is a word that you add to a Note – with a 'hashtag' in front of it.

A tag acts as a categorization of your Note, and more than one Tag can be added anywhere in your Note. This then allows you to search for Notes that have a single Tag or a combination of Tags.

In the screenshot on the below, the **HTML Label** Note has the tags **website** and **coding** (shown in yellow text), in this case added at the top under the Note name (but they could have been added anywhere in the note).

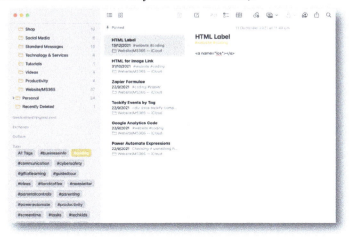

A quick look at the Notes App

The Notes sidebar includes a Tags section, and you can choose one or more tags to see the Notes that include the set of tags that you select.

The image above shows the list of Notes I get when I select the **#coding** Tag in the left sidebar.

If I click the **#website** tag as well, I get just those Notes that have both selected tags.

As you can see from my list of tags shown above (which were just set up to demonstrate the feature), you can easily end up with a very long list of tags.

So, try to be a bit frugal with the number that you set up.

And clean up any you no longer need (which involves removing the Tag from each of the Notes in which it appears).

Quick Notes

I love this feature that arrived in macOS Monterey (also available on iPads). It is the Quick Note feature, which allows you to really quickly jot down a Note without having to open the Notes app first.

Hover your mouse pointer down at the **bottom right of the Mac's screen**, and you will see the corner of a Note appear.

Click on this to start a Quick Note.

In **Notes -> Settings**, the **Resume last Quick Note** option allows you to make the choice of whether your previous Quick Note is resumed when you start a Quick Note, or whether a new Quick Note is started each time.

Quick Notes can then be found in their own section at the top of the Notes sidebar.

These Quick Notes can then be dragged into another folder or, if they are no longer required, deleted.

A quick look at the Notes App

Add App Link

Quite often, it is a link to something else that you are wanting to add to a Note.

For example, perhaps you have a web page open and want the link for that web page to be added to your current Note.

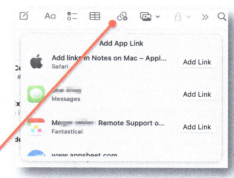

Or perhaps you want to link your Note to a Message, or a Calendar event.

There is now a new icon that appears in the Notes Toolbar when you are creating/editing a Note – a link symbol that allows the adding of such a link.

When this link symbol is clicked, the list of options that appear will be dependent on what else is open on your Mac.

As an example, I have a couple of web pages open in Safari and on Chrome – so these appear as options in the image on the previous page.

I also have a Messages conversation open, and my Fantastical app has a particular even highlighted.

I can choose to **Add Link** for any of these items.

In the example on the right, I chose the first Add Link in the list – which has added a link to a particular article that I was reading in Safari.

Other new features for Notes in macOS Ventura

Smart Folders enhanced

Smart Folders have gotten smarter in macOS Ventura. Previously, they could only be based on Tags.

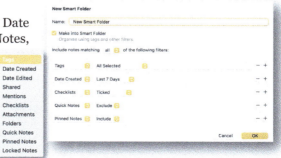

Now they can be based on Date Created, Date Modified, Shared Notes, those with Mentions, Checklists, Attachments, based on folder, Quick Notes, Pinned Notes and Locked Note. Rules can use any combination of these.

A quick look at the Notes App

There is also now the option to choose whether the Notes in the Smart Folder must match 'All' or just Any' of the filters.

Grouping of Notes list by Date

Notes can now be grouped by date in the preview list – as Today, Previous 7 Days, Previous 30 Days, Year.

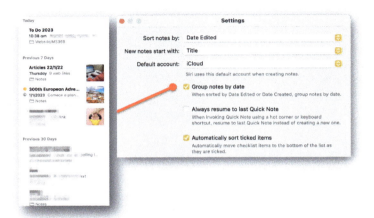

This can be turned off in **Notes -> Settings**.

Quick Filters on Search

The Search option at top right now allows you to filter your Notes quickly and easily, to just show particular types of Notes or notes with particular features.

The image below shows the list of Filters available.

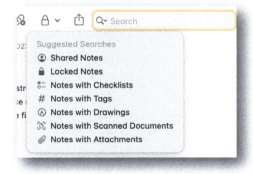

Other Books in this Series

A Guided Tour

Files, Folders & Finder

All Sorts of Handy Tips

The Photos App

Videos about the Mac

Learn even more about your Mac with a range of Videos about the Mac, available on the iTandCoffee website.

For more information about iTandCoffee class videos and user guides, visit

www.itandcoffee.com.au/videos

www.itandcoffee.com.au/guides